A souvenir guide

Gunby Estate, Hall and Gardens

Lincolnshire

Andrew Barber

National Trust

'A Haunt of Ancient Peace'

'… an English home, gray twilight pour'd
On dewy pastures, dewy trees
Softer than sleep – all things in order stored,
A haunt of ancient peace.'

Alfred, Lord Tennyson

A signed manuscript scrap quoting this famous quatrain hangs in the Entrance Hall at Gunby. The poet Tennyson was born locally and befriended the squire of Gunby when they were at school together at Louth and later at Cambridge. The lines are his and are believed to be a description of Gunby. Certainly their drowsy, timeless quality is matched by the calm, almost other-worldliness of this out-of-the-way place.

The quintessence of Englishness

Gunby is a place that seems to have inspired happiness and great content in its people – although very often expressed most poignantly and forcefully when at great distance: Peregrine Langton-Massingberd, the consort of the early 19th-century owner, bemoaned his enforced (and frequent) absences from the place. His wayward grandson, 'Naughty' Algernon, reflected fondly when contemplating permanent exile enforced by debt: '… but that Gunby & England would hold my affections as the place of my birth & the land of my fathers there is every reason to believe….' At times of war it is where thoughts flew: '… I think I have crammed more concentrated delight and happiness into my visit to Gunby than in any other place' wrote Peter Montgomery in a letter to Lady Montgomery-Massingberd, 19 October 1943. For James Lees-Milne it was the quintessence of Englishness, and its rescue was as much an act of patriotism as fighting in the war itself.

Cultural connections

Gunby is a place of connections. Despite its remote location, the house has been the focus of consistently fascinating groups of friends and contacts throughout its history: from Dr Johnson in the 18th century to Rudyard Kipling in the 20th, from Charles Darwin to Josiah Wedgwood, Holman Hunt to Virginia Woolf, Edward Lear to Vaughan Williams and King Haakon to Hubert Parry, the list is as long as it is various.

A haven for wildlife

Set in the flat lands on the southern tip of the Lincolnshire Wolds, much of the estate for much of its history has been marsh. Effective drainage made it into rich farmland but what could have been a wealthy agricultural estate was crippled by mis-management and subsequent sales that left it too small an entity to flourish. The patchwork of small blocks of woodland, numerous ponds and agricultural fields that remains today provides a living for three farm tenants. It is a haven for important wildlife such as the endangered Great Crested Newt and various species of invertebrate that live in standing deadwood, for which the park is, selectively, managed.

Exemplary tenants

Management of the house and gardens by the National Trust has followed ownership by nearly 70 years. For 40 of the intervening years the house and gardens were cared for in exemplary fashion by the latest in a long line of tenants to have occupied Gunby throughout its history. Now the opportunity has arisen for visitors to see more of the property than ever before. Over the next decade the rich social, archaeological and natural history of Gunby will be investigated and interpreted for visitors so that something new will always be here to be discovered.

Above The entrance front from the north-west. The north wing (two-storey block on the left) was added in 1873 and 1898

Far left The Gunby scrap-screen was created by Sir Archibald Montgomery-Massingberd in his retirement after 1936

Left Amateur theatricals at Gunby in 1891; photographed by L. Lane Fox

The first Massingberds

'...[in] descent, patrimony, ample estate and ingenious education, every way answerable....'

From the preamble to the letters patent of Oliver Cromwell conferring a baronetcy on Sir Henry Massingberd in 1658.

Above St Peter's church, Gunby (not NT), stands in the park to the south-east of the house. It was rebuilt in 1868–70, replacing a Georgian church

The Massingberd family is long established in Lincolnshire, tracing its descent to Lambert Massingberd of Sutterton, who was convicted of grievous bodily harm in Boston in 1288. Through the marriage of Sir Thomas Massingberd to Joan de Bratoft in 1495 the lands of Bratoft and Gunby and the moated manor house at Bratoft came into the family, surrounded by fish ponds and an extensive park. An Elizabethan garden seems to have adorned this dwelling, of which archaeological remains are still evident in the landscape today.

Human habitation at both Bratoft and Gunby goes back to long before the Massingberds arrived: deserted medieval villages are evident in the archaeology of both Gunby and Bratoft parks, whilst recent archaeological investigation suggests that an early Iron Age site, which is thought to have been of some significance due to its scale and to the large amount of burnt deposits found, sits under the gardens of the Hall and extends out into the Glebe Field to the east.

Of the wider Massingberd family, the younger son of Sir Thomas, Sir Oswald Massingberd, served as Grand Prior of Ireland in the Sovereign Military Order of Malta from 1547, where he was arraigned for the murder of four slaves (the product of the privateering operations for which the Knights of Malta became notorious in the 16th and 17th centuries) and conspiracy to murder the Grand Master.

During the Civil War the Massingberd brothers, Henry and Drayner, fought on the Parliamentary side. Both brothers prospered under the Commonwealth of Oliver Cromwell. Drayner went on to found the branch of the family seated at South Ormsby in Lincolnshire, whilst Henry served as High Sheriff of the county and was rewarded with a baronetcy by Cromwell, not least because of his generosity to the State in maintaining 30 foot soldiers in Ireland for three years to keep the peace after the bloody campaigns of 1649–51. For reasons that are not entirely clear, Sir Henry managed the unusual feat of having his Cromwellian baronetcy reconferred by Charles II in 1660.

It was Sir Henry's son, Sir William, the second baronet, who decided to move the family seat across the fields from Bratoft to Gunby.

Right The tomb brass of Sir Thomas Massingberd and Joan de Bratoft in Gunby church, c.1400

Far right The coat of arms of Sir Henry Massingberd, who was created baronet in 1660

Henry Massingbeard of Bratosts Hall in the County of Lincolne Esq.ʳ Created Baronet

The builder Sir William Massingberd

From contemporary references it seems likely that Sir William was building on the site of an existing manor house, but nothing of it remains today. Some of the bricks used to build the house were quarried from the old manor house at Bratoft which Sir William dismantled. Many more were made on site by a T. Pain, who was paid for making bricks and for 'setting ye clamp' in 1696. Further payments for 'deals' (structural timbers and panelling) imported through Hull from Holland and later for brass locks, latches and hinges – many of which are still in evidence on the doors in the house – are recorded in the family papers. In April 1701 the glazing of some of the windows in the Hall was accounted, and Mr Price of Holborn in London was paid for Crown glass for 23 windows containing 24 squares in each window and 6 windows containing 28 squares at 9d per square 'whereof a penny a Square was for putty...'.

The result is a four-square, no-nonsense brick house relieved by sparing use of stone for quoins and window surrounds and the subtlety of raised brick panels in the parapet. Its plan internally is equally straightforward: two main reception rooms set back to back centrally with four smaller rooms at each angle separated at either end by staircases. The first and second floors introduce a corridor running the length between the staircases with chambers symmetrically disposed about. Decoration is minimal, but every room is panelled and provided with generous fireplaces. Everything speaks of quality, well found and finished, but never falling into luxury or excess.

Sir William served as High Sheriff for Bedfordshire in 1694 and seems to have maintained his family's eminence in Lincolnshire also. His namesake bachelor son, who succeeded him briefly from 1719–23, was MP for Lincolnshire. Thereafter the family trait of female succession began with Elizabeth, daughter of the builder and wife of Mr Meux, inheriting and joining her maiden name to that of her husband. Her son, William Meux Massingberd held Gunby for a lengthy tenure (1738–80) and built the stable yard to the north of the house. He married twice and had many children by his second marriage, but only one son, who predeceased him, by his first. His grandson Henry succeeded him, but lived

Above Sir William Massingberd, 2nd Bt (1649–1719), who built the present house

Right William Meux Massingberd (1703–81)

Far right Sir William Massingberd, 3rd Bt (1677–1723)

Above right Gunby from the west c.1735

away from Gunby, which was let to a succession of tenants. Curiously, it is the absentee Henry's bookplate that appears in many of the volumes in the Library. This collection is considered one of the finest small-scale squire's libraries in the care of the National Trust.

On Henry's death, which occurred in France in 1784, his baby daughter, Elizabeth Mary Anne, succeeded. Gunby continued to be let whilst she was brought up by a coterie of aunts and great-aunts in and around Lincolnshire.

'…. the Hall is … robust, unostentatious, dignified and a trifle prim….'
James Lees-Milne, *People and Places*, 1992

The planter Peregrine Langton Massingberd

Opposite Peregrine Langton
Massingberd (d.1856)

Right Gunby from the
south-west; watercolour
by Peregrine Langton
Massingberd c.1810

In 1802 Elizabeth Mary Anne Massingberd married Peregrine Langton, second son of Bennet Langton of Langton in Lincolnshire. Peregrine left copious quantities of letters, journals and, uniquely, a book in which he recorded all tree planting on the estate. The Gunby Tree Book, together with his journals and letters, give a glimpse of life at Gunby and abroad as Peregrine struggled with a tempestuous marriage (which eventually broke down), his children (all of whom either died or otherwise disappointed him), money (the lack of which forced him out of Gunby) and religion (which overtook him forcefully and irrevocably during a storm in the South Atlantic).

The gloomy image of the place conjured by Lord Torrington's terse description must have been banished fairly quickly by the arrival of seven children over the seventeen years following their marriage and by Peregrine's planting and Elizabeth's devising. A charming notebook of hers contains designs for a rose garden, planted to the south of the house (where the old tennis court is now) and for a pretty *cottage ornée* which was built – twice – as a gate lodge (superseded by the current lodge in 1908) and on the estate. Her proposals to add an Italianate tower to the south-east corner of the house, however, remained unexecuted.

The trouble was that she and her husband seldom agreed. In 1814 on returning from one of his trips abroad, Peregrine noted in his journal: '... my dearest wife, being thoroughly disgusted with the forlorn appearance...the gardens made had them all improved.... The Ha!Ha! which I had dug she filled up and threw

'... this house, tho' well placed and with wood in view ... is a most melancholy place: suicide in every room...'

John Byng, Viscount Torrington, *A Tour into Lincolnshire*, 1791

a broad ... gravel walk, instead of the one near the house which I had made, at a much greater distance....'. Gunby was Elizabeth's inheritance (on their marriage Peregrine had taken the name of Massingberd with that of Langton), and Peregrine, for all his assumption of the squire's place, had to defer to her. This subversion of normal practice must have placed the marriage under unbearable pressure. Elizabeth went to live abroad, at Versailles and then Mannheim, leaving some of the children with Peregrine. He was unable to afford to live at Gunby and wandered the country (and the world, taking two of his daughters out to Australia in an abortive attempt to find a new life there), eventually settling in the Lodge at Gunby, where he kept bees, whilst the Hall was let to tenants.

'Naughty' Algernon

The Reverend Algernon Langton-Massingberd, eldest son of Peregrine and Elizabeth Mary Anne, had only one child, also named Algernon (and called 'Naughty' in the family annals for reasons that will become apparent). The little boy grew up largely untutored and untamed. '… little Alge is allowed to run wild, & hunt the lambs… in the Park,' Peregrine wrote disapprovingly in his journal. His wild and erratic nature, which remained unimproved by brief sojourns at school in Blackheath and in the households of several clergymen (including, in his grandfather's dyspeptic scribble, '…that rank Pusey-ite [Archdeacon] Dennison…') was given some boundaries when his parents bought him a commission as a midshipman in the Royal Navy. He served his teenage years on the China seas maintaining supplies, cleanliness and discipline on board. Unsurprisingly, he took the opportunity offered by his father's untimely death in 1844 to quit the Navy and travel (with his mother), witnessing the overthrow of Louis-Philippe in France. By 1848 he had resumed a military career, this time as a junior officer in the Dragoons, followed, at his majority in 1849 – and amidst ox roasts and a massive dinner for all his Gunby tenantry – by a move to the Royal Regiment of Horse Guards. In this role he began to enjoy life to the full, taking a house in fashionable Eaton Square and becoming involved in gambling rings and murky horse dealing. Also he began to take an interest in radical politics.

Algernon wrote ecstatically of his meeting with Louis Kossuth, the Hungarian revolutionary. They had met in Turkey after the failure of the short-lived Hungarian republic. Thus it was natural that Algernon should put his house in London at Kossuth's disposal when the revolutionary visited England late in 1851. Kossuth travelled the country making speeches. The Government remained mute but, after Kossuth's departure for America, took revenge on those who had helped him. Algernon was required to resign his commission and, with no position and hounded by creditors, he too departed for America early in 1852, never to return. His travels took him to Havana, Australia, New York and Lima in Peru where his last contact is recorded *c*.1854.

During this time Gunby was tenanted once more by a solicitor and his family, the Hollways. Algernon's career from 1852 until his death in 1855 is charted by the investigations of his indefatigable uncle Charles and a precious cache of three letters that survive in his hand.

'My Byron, Bible, & old scrap book I shall require at your hands –'

The last surviving message written by Algernon Massingberd before he disappeared without trace in 1854.

Revolution in Europe

1848 saw a series of violent uprisings against the *anciens regimes* of Europe. The French monarchy was finally extinguished and various Italian and German states (neither country was yet united) toppled their rulers. The massive Austro-Hungarian empire too was shaken to its core. Hungary rose in revolt and established a short-lived republic. One of its leaders, a charismatic revolutionary named Louis Kossuth aroused great sympathy across Europe for Hungary's cause. However, he was regarded as a dangerous revolutionary by many governments, including the British.

Above left The Rev. Algernon Langton Massingberd (1804–44)

Opposite 'Naughty Algernon' Massingberd (1828–55)

Above right 'Naughty Algernon', aged seven; marble bust by Charles Physick, 1835

The consolidator
Charles Langton Massingberd

Charles was the youngest son of Peregrine and Elizabeth Mary Anne Massingberd. Having served a spell in the Austrian army he married and settled to life as a gentleman, unconscious of the danger into which the irrepressible vigour of his nephew Algernon's enthusiasm for adventure had placed the family's fortunes.

Algernon abandoned plans to build a trading station on Lake Nicaragua: '…The Capital I should require wd. be 1800£ or 2000. with this I should go out & purchase an estate of 2000 acres – wilderness woods & water – in the vicinity of the River S. Juan. build a small quay. & there erect a log hut. 6 German labourers would accompany me…') Having taken to speculation in the import–export of sewing machines, Algernon had fled from his creditors to Sydney, ending up trading silver and guns with the native tribes of Peru. Here the trail his uncle was following in pursuit of proof of Algernon's death, went cold, until rumours began to circulate of a party of Americans, Mexicans and Europeans fighting a pitched battle with Brazilian soldiers on the border in 1855. Due to his habit of using aliases (to throw creditors off his trail) and the lack of a body (none has been found to this day), it was impossible for a long time to prove Algernon's presence at the skirmish. However, a survivor carried a sophisticated rifle of a type known to have been owned by Algernon. This evidence – and much more amassed by Charles – was enough, eventually,

Scarborough bought much and subsequently developed the resort of Skegness on part of it.

Charles was an acute businessman and had invested well, amongst other things in the development of the railway network. Having paid off all his nephew's debts and confirmed his right to inherit Gunby, Charles was in a position to make the first major alterations to the Hall since it was built. In 1873 he added a two-storey wing to the north of the house, providing better service accommodation, secondary bedrooms and a new dining room. He installed plumbing, bringing the luxury of running water and plumbed lavatories to the house.

Genial, musical and an accomplished artist, Charles was much in demand at parties for his fine tenor singing voice. To the end of his life he retained the engaging habit of slipping into German, sometimes in the middle of sentences; a relic of his youth spent on the Continent. His delicate constitution led him to spend much of his later life in the beneficial climate of Bournemouth, where his daughter, Emily had built a house.

Left Charles Langton Massingberd (1815–87)

Above Harriet Langton Massingberd; painted in Rome in 1842

Bottom right A Viennese table water set decorated with the monogram of Harriet Massingberd

to convince the High Court that Algernon was dead and to release Gunby from the legal entanglement of Chancery.

This was concluded only in 1862. In the meantime, on top of Algernon's incontinent spending, further sales had to be undertaken to satisfy creditors. The family portraits and principal furniture were saved only by the action of John Hollway, the tenant, who bought them and later sold them back to Charles. In the end the estate was reduced to a fraction of its former size; the Earl of

The campaigner Emily Langton Massingberd

Charles Langton Massingberd had two daughters. The elder, Emily Caroline, grew up to become one of the most distinctive characters in the Massingberd line.

Emily was a teetotal political activist who campaigned for women's rights and, for preference, dressed like a man. She was a keen amateur actor (preferring to take male parts) and played the violin. She had a passionate (if unconsummated) love affair with one cousin whilst she was married to another. She had four children.

Her ethical and political beliefs were united in the Pioneer Club, an institution she founded in 1892 (see box). Whilst the story of her lecturing her tenantry on the evils of drink from a boat moored in Ice House Pond may be apocryphal, her lifelong hatred of alcohol had effects on Gunby that survive to this day. Massingberd Arms Farm started life as a pub which Emily converted into a Temperance House, whereupon it went bankrupt and became a farmhouse. In the Hall her youngest daughter, as zealous as her mother, but married to a soldier who liked to drink, destroyed the Library to create a Sitting Room in which drink could be taken whilst preserving the teetotal purity of her Withdrawing Room (see below p.30).

The 1888 Local Government Reform Act increased the franchise but left vague who had the right to stand for election and who did not. Thus in the elections of January 1889 Emily stood for the ward of Partney, in her right as a landowner, and lost by only 20 votes. She was one of the first women in the country to stand for public office. General female emancipation was not enacted until 1918.

Emily, who had been widowed in 1875, succeeded her father at Gunby in 1887. She enjoyed the life of a country squire up to a point, but found the isolation of Lincolnshire trying and, after a couple of years, let Gunby and retired to live in Bournemouth once more (where she produced amateur theatricals with her friend Agnes Mangles) and London. Here she preferred to live at the Club in Bruton Street rather than with her teenaged children in the house she rented for them in Kensington Square.

Top Emily with her violin

Right Emily Langton Massingberd (1847–97)

Far right Banner embroidered with the initials ELMC ('East Lindsey Music Club')

Known in the family as 'Munny', she was charmingly vague; writing to Stephen, her only son, to congratulate him on his engagement: '… Fardie was 26 when he married. You are 25 aren't you? How pleased and delighted he would have been….' and sometimes disarmingly honest too; to a friend describing her own fiancé on their engagement she confided: '... he is very slight and fair, not nice-looking I suppose, though of course I think him delightful in every way….'

She died after an operation in 1897 aged only 49.

The Pioneer Club

A socially levelling institution for women (men were permitted only at Social Evenings on Wednesdays) where all were identified by number rather than by name, it sought through lectures (every Thursday) and social campaigning to tackle issues of concern such as vivisection and explore new philosophies such as theosophy, but overwhelmingly it was concerned with improving the lot of women.

Stephen Massingberd and the Lushingtons

'Stephen is quite the country gentleman, going to Sessions & County Committees & shooting…'

Vernon Lushington to his daughter Susan, 9 October 1904

Stephen moved to Gunby in 1898 shortly after his mother's death, inaugurating a golden epoch that was to survive both World Wars and the transfer of Gunby to the National Trust in 1944. Stephen was newly married to a beautiful, artistic young wife. Together they were to transform the local musical scene, introducing singing competitions throughout the county, training choirs and orchestras, performing concerts and operettas and bringing first-class music to this remote corner of Lincolnshire. The tenor Gervase Elwes, of a Lincolnshire family, made the decision to become a professional singer in the Music Room at Gunby.

Margaret, Stephen's wife, was one of three daughters of Vernon and Jane Lushington. After their mother's early death, the three, Katherine (known as Kitty), Margaret and Susan looked after their father in 36 Kensington Square whilst the young Massingberds kept house at no. 42. A close friendship developed between the three Lushington girls and the three Massingberd girls very largely centring on music (although Mildred, Stephen's elder sister, could never see the point of it). It was a mutual love of the 'cello that drew Stephen and Margaret together.

Vernon Lushington had always had artistic sympathies; it was in his college rooms that the historic first meeting took place between Dante Gabriel Rossetti and the young Edward Burne-Jones. Latterly he had supported and patronised the work of the Pre-Raphaelite artist Arthur Hughes, who portrayed the female members of the Lushington family in a musical ensemble called *The Home Quartette*. The spirit of this late 19th-century explosion of artistic endeavour pervades Gunby still, from the 'Daisy' wallpaper by William Morris & Co. on the stairs to the occasional pieces of Aesthetic furniture and the massive sepia photographs of Renaissance masterpieces to be found in the bedrooms.

Margaret loved gardening. During her time, the formal yew allées on the west front of the house were planted and the pervasive influence of roses in the garden, although greatly augmented by Betty Wrisdale in more recent times, seems to have started with Margaret. She is depicted in the garden at Gunby in her portrait by Arthur Hughes.

Margaret died of peritonitis in 1906. Whilst the musical traditions that had been laid down by her drive and energy were taken up and continued by her sister Susan with Stephen's younger sister, Diana, Stephen never remarried and, although he survived the First World War on active service, he died, childless, at the relatively young age of 56 in 1925.

Bottom left *The Home Quartette*; by Arthur Hughes. The Lushington women were all very musical

Top left Stephen Massingberd (1869–1925) with his sister Mary (1871–1950)

Top right Margaret Lushington (d.1906), who married Stephen Langton Massingberd; painted by Arthur Hughes in the garden at Gunby, which she loved

The benefactors
Field Marshal Sir Archibald and Lady Montgomery-Massingberd

Stephen's elder sister, Mildred, did not enjoy being a country landowner, preferring to live privately in the house she had built with her husband (and second cousin) Leonard Darwin in the New Forest. So, as her next sister Mary had married the heir to an estate in Northern Ireland, Gunby came to the youngest, Diana. She had married Archibald Montgomery, the younger brother of her sister Mary's husband. Known in the family as Archie, obligingly he followed tradition and took his wife's name when she inherited Gunby.

Archie was a successful career soldier. He had served in the Boer War, making friends with Rudyard Kipling. He started the First World War as a Major, rising to the rank of Major General by the Armistice. He was recognised as a brilliant strategist and wrote the history of the campaign 'the Hundred Days' that brought the war to a close. He was appointed Chief of the Imperial General Staffs in 1933 and became Field Marshal in 1935. Thus he was in charge of the entire army. He wrote an important pamphlet *The Future Re-Organization of the British Army* in 1935, which foresaw the cataclysm to come with remarkable prescience.

Left Field Marshal Sir Archibald Montgomery-Massingberd; painted by Sir Oswald Birley

Top right Diana Langton Massingberd, who married Archibald Montgomery in 1896; painted by Richard Ziegler in 1943

Bottom right The riding boots were worn by Sir Archibald Montgomery-Massingberd

Diana was a strict teetotaller and, like her mother, she was a fine musician. As a teenager, she had sung in a madrigal group in London with the Lushingtons. Known as 'The Magpies' because of their black and white dress, they sang at charity concerts and society events. On one memorable occasion in 1893 they sang in the garden of Sir Charles Stanford the composer to his guests, who included the composers Bruch, Saint-Saens and Tchaikovsky. Ralph Vaughan Williams was a cousin who dedicated songs to her. She had a clear, sweet soprano singing voice, and was a conductor as well as an accomplished player of the violin and viola (which she always pronounced with the accent on the first syllable!).

Archie died in 1947, but Diana lived on into extreme old age, a tall, erect figure still graceful enough to attract wolf-whistles from soldiers (to the officer of men in the park after the war she remarked; '… will you kindly inform your men that I may look 18 from the back, but I am 80 at the front!').

'They are such dear people …
I would walk to the ends of the earth
to help them.'

James Lees-Milne,
diary entry for Thursday 25 March 1943

The last battle

In 1943 Diana and Archie faced their greatest challenge. When the Field Marshal found men marking up trees for felling he was told that the Air Ministry had ordered it – and the demolition of the house – to facilitate heavily-laden bombers on the neighbouring airfield. Archie lobbied everyone (including the King) to prevent this 'act of vandalism'. When criticised for being unpatriotic he pointed out that Hitler was destroying enough beautiful buildings already without needlessly adding more. Eventually the point was won and the house saved. In thanksgiving Archie and Diana decided to offer the entire estate to the National Trust. This act of great generosity was finally achieved in the following year.

Gunby and the nation

Hugh Montgomery-Massingberd has left a sad description of Gunby in the final years of his great-aunt Diana's tenure. Visiting in 1962 as a teenager, filled with romantic notions of country house life, he found the atmosphere of Gunby stultifying, with the blind nonagenarian chatelaine ruled by her harridan housekeeper, Mrs Sheehan-Hunt. Hugh's own attempts to use Gunby as a weekend retreat from his law studies in London are chronicled, hilariously, in this memoir *Daydream Believer*, complete with a pantomime caretaker, Rogers, employed after his retirement from Crumlin Road gaol by Hugh's father, John Montgomery-Massingberd.

Finding the financial burden of the tenancy at Gunby too great whilst working for the BBC in London, John sub-let Gunby to the Lincolnshire farmer Jack Wrisdale in 1967, releasing the full tenancy to him in 1976. For the next 40 years, Jack and his wife Betty made Gunby their home, bringing up their family here and caring for the place in exemplary fashion. Opening to the public just one afternoon a week, the house was less of a draw than the garden (open two days a week, and certain weekends for the benefit of local charities).

Opposite **Hugh Montgomery-Massingberd** (1946–2007), who helped to revive the art of the newspaper obituary

Right **Betty Wrisdale**, who did so much to create the garden at Gunby today

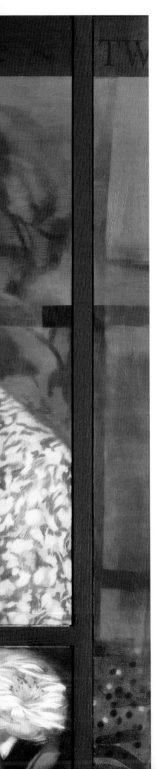

In the revival of the gardens, after the decline of John Montgomery-Massingberd's absentee tenancy, Betty Wrisdale's interest and skill as a gardener were crucial. Her understanding of plants and innate feeling for colour and form were fundamental to how the garden was restored and to how it appears still today. Together Jack and Betty restored the house, redecorating much of the interior and, repeating the generosity of earlier tenants, buying indigenous contents when the family was forced to sell, and conveying them to the National Trust when they retired so that everything remains at Gunby today.

When the Wrisdales left Gunby in 2007, they were succeeded in the tenancy by Dr and Mrs Ayres who had family connections with the Massingberds through Dr Ayres's great-great-aunt, who had been nurse and nanny to Stephen, Mildred, Mary and Diana in the later 19th century. Sadly, their tenancy was cut short by the tragic death of Dr Ayres in a car crash in 2010. After an interval the National Trust decided to take on the direct management of Gunby. This will involve the gradual development of necessary visitor services which the National Trust intends to achieve over the coming years. In the meantime, the house and gardens are open more fully now and for a longer season than ever before. In this new guidebook a more detailed guide to both is offered.

Exploring Gunby

'The stark skyline without any frills or furbelows seemed fitting for the residence of a couple who epitomized the Tory axiom of Crown and Church.'

James Lees-Milne, *People and Places*, 1992

The Exterior

To get a proper perspective on this most strait-laced of English country houses, you need to view it from the formal garden to the west. From here the severe symmetry of the original design is most clearly seen. The central bay containing the front door is recessed between the two identical wings. Decoration is almost entirely absent save for the flourish of the carved arms and date over the door and the brick panels in relief in each bay of the parapet. The effect of the architecture is entirely in the rhythm of the bays (two windows to each wing, three to the centre) and the contrast of the plainly moulded stone string courses, window surrounds and quoins within the sea of subtle variations of colour in the brick. The strong horizontal of the parapet forbids any thought of dramatic verticality. All is refinement and restraint; the enjoyment of minute detail and subtle contrast is what Gunby offers to those who look.

Also from this western viewpoint the extension of 1873 (and further extension by two bays in 1898) can be seen to best advantage. Copying the main features of the old house, the two-storey extension sits over its basement tactfully in the shadow of its older sibling. Only the intrusion of plate-glass sashes in the ground-floor windows has had to be 'corrected' by the introduction of hinged wooden frets internally (look out for these in the Music Room).

On the south front, where the flower garden stood historically, the two ground-floor windows are later insertions, introduced when the Hall and Library were combined to create a single 'living-hall'. The triple 'Venetian' window lights the main staircase and is an unexpected flourish. It is not part of the original design and may be the work of William Meux Massingberd c.1735. The oval openings just below the parapet are probably owl holes, encouraging predators to roost in the roof space and thereby discourage vermin.

The clay substrate at Gunby causes movement in prolonged periods of drought, the effects of which are evident in the façade of the east front, where the stone string course wobbles alarmingly.

On the north front note the introduction of a pair of arched windows just to the left of the door and wonder, perhaps, why?

Opposite The west and south fronts

Above The entrance front from the west

In some of the Basement windows at Gunby are examples of the true use of 'bottle' glass – the slightly raised centre of the crown glass plate from which all window glass was cut in the late 17th century. This was the most distorted part of the plate, and thus the least useful, but economy dictated that it should not be wasted, so the crown centres were put into windows where light, rather than clarity or uniformity, was the priority.

The Interior
The Music Room
The Ante Room

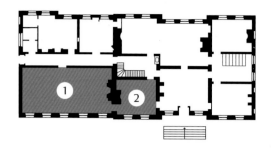

1. The Music Room

Running the full length of the west front of the 1873 wing, this room only came into existence in its current form in 1898, when the wing was extended a further two bays to the north, and the oak panelling with its complex mouldings was installed, a wedding present to Stephen and Margaret Massingberd from her father.

It was in this room that Diana Massingberd coached her string ensembles and here that singers sang and choirs rehearsed. The grand piano, specially strengthened against the rigours of intercontinental travel, went out to India with Diana and Archie on his postings there.

Hot posset

Posset is a confection of cream, sugar, eggs, spices and sherry served warm and consumed as a divided curd. It was popular in the late 17th century, when the two delft pots here were made, probably in England. The curd was eaten with a spoon from the top and the alcoholic whey drunk through the tube at the bottom as the pot was passed round the table.

2. The Ante Room

Entering the old house into what was formerly the Housekeeper's Room, with a flagged floor, this became an Ante room to the new Dining Room as part of the alterations of 1873.

Opposite The Gunby String Players in the Music Room in 1952. Lady Montgomery-Massingberd is visible on the far left playing the viola

Top left Bennet Langton was the father of Peregrine Langton Massingberd; portrait by Joshua Reynolds

Portraits

Over the piano hang the portraits by Reynolds of Bennet Langton and his wife Mary, Dowager Countess of Rothes. Their second son, Peregrine, married the heiress of Gunby in 1802. Bennet was a great friend of James Boswell, the biographer of Samuel Johnson. An appealing character, he read Johnson's Dictionary to his family at breakfast – a meal that seems to have taken half the morning to complete – whilst his servant combed his long, unpowdered hair. Through this connection the later Massingberds were related to the Wedgwood and Darwin families, both of great significance in the industrial and scientific development of this country.

Ceramics

Gunby has a fine collection of delft pottery, much of it gathered in this room; the fancy-shaped jars are Dutch and were made for display as a garniture on a mantelpiece, whilst the two posset pots are rare survivals.

Pictures

A watercolour of the house in Kensington Square where the young Massingberds lived in the 1890s hangs on the left, and a study of a moss rose by the celebrated garden designer Alfred Parsons hangs on the right. Hugh Norris, a Lushington cousin, imagined the darkly foreboding bluebell wood in the painting above the chest-on-chest.

Furniture

This chest-on-chest is one of the finest pieces of 18th-century English furniture at Gunby; the quality of the walnut veneers and of the original brass handles is excellent, whilst the natural proportions of the graduated drawers and of the simple mouldings is entirely satisfying.

   The other major piece of furniture in the room is the walnut escritoire or fall-front desk. Dating from *c.*1710, this piece had been altered to form a cupboard with a pair of side-hung doors in the upper part. It was restored to its original form by Mr and Mrs Wrisdale during the period in which they owned it.

The Entrance Hall

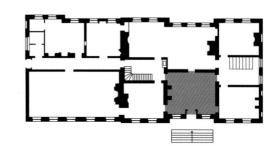

Below The Entrance Hall

Right A decorative brass fingerplate in the Entrance Hall

In 1926, the wall between the Entrance Hall and the Library was removed to create a large 'sitting-hall' and the books scattered about the house (and some of the more untidy ones burned). The odd proportions of the hybrid room that resulted, created to facilitate the taking of alcohol by guests in an otherwise teetotal house, are best appreciated here.

In the once-more symmetrical hall, the builder, Sir William Massingberd, dominates again from his portrait (by Riley) over the mantel. Below, between two watercolour portraits of the Revd. Algernon Massingberd and his sister Mary Neville, hangs a frame containing four lines of manuscript. This precious scrap is signed by the local poet Alfred Tennyson. The lines are from his epic poem *The Palace of Art* and are believed to describe Gunby, which Tennyson knew well. In one of the family scrapbooks is a faint pencil sketch by his friend Algernon Massingberd, showing the poet as a gangling young man, all quiff and cravat, smoking his long-shafted clay pipe.

Portraits

A gallery of family portraits: Mrs Meux (in the curious octagonal frame) who succeeded her bachelor brother, the last baronet; her son William, in a portrait by Reynolds ruined by over-cleaning, and his son Thomas, who predeceased his father. Thomas's widow, Elizabeth, was Lord Byron's landlady at no. 16 Piccadilly in the early 19th century, leading the young poet into bad ways with money lenders.

Beside the front door is a tiny sepia ink sketch entitled, inimitably, 'Ko Ko Nut Parms'. It is from the pen of Edward Lear the jolly lyricist and populariser of the limerick who was a family friend. On the opposite side of the front door is a little portrait of James Boswell, the biographer of Dr Samuel Johnson, by Peregrine Langton's brother, George. On the evidence of this, George was a better artist than his brother.

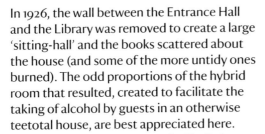

The reeded doorcases with their distinctive lions' masks are part of the modernising touches instituted by Elizabeth Mary Anne Massingberd, the grand-daughter of Elizabeth (Byron's landlady) and the wife of Peregrine Langton.

The Library

This is considered to be – the remains of – one of the best examples of a squire's library to survive. Largely collected between 1690 and 1730, the books '… in their modest way … are a remarkable and vivid testament to the vibrancy of cultural life in a remote corner of Georgian England.' (P. Hoare, Library report, 2002). However, they have had a chequered history.

Portraits

Inset in the panelling over the fireplace is the portrait of the last Massingberd baronet, who died young in 1723, but not before he had made an impact as an industrious MP.

The other portrait in the room, between the windows, is of Betty Wrisdale, who lived at Gunby from 1967 to 2007. She and her husband laboured hard in the planning and restoration of the gardens. Her careful custodianship of the property is referenced in the marginal panels of this portrait.

Ceramics

A Wedgwood plaque of *The Dancing Hours* was a wedding present to Archie and Diana Montgomery from Godfrey Wedgwood, who was a cousin of Diana.

Above the bookcase on the wall opposite the fireplace is part of a Chinese porcelain dinner service, made for export to Europe in the late 18th century. It was re-assembled here in 1998 after the wall was rebuilt with the help of money from the sale of books belonging to James Lees-Milne. It had long been the ambition of Betty Wrisdale to see the wall put back and the proportions of the two rooms restored.

Above The Gunby copy of Boswell's *Life of Johnson* is inscribed by the author to Bennet Langton, who was a friend

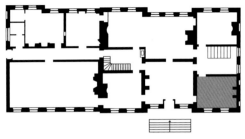

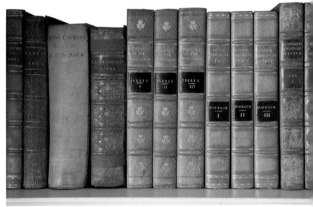

Clock

The bracket clock has inlay and castings that illustrate the short-lived 'Egyptian' taste that swept decorative art after the invasion of Egypt by Napoleon at the very end of the 18th century. Napoleon's artist Denon provided drawings of the sphinx, pyramids and other pharoanic objects to the Sèvres factory, and the craze spread all across Europe.

Sculpture

The marble bust is of 'Naughty' Algernon. Who, from this, would guess at the career he was to have?

Left **The Library**

Above **Gunby has one of the best surviving examples of an early 18th-century squire's library**

The Oak Staircase
The Study

1. The Oak Staircase

The staircase, with its triple-twisted slender balusters, is dated by Nikolaus Pevsner the architectural historian to c.1730. Together with the Venetian window, plaster panelling and cornice, he attributes this space to William Meux Massingberd. There is no documentary evidence for this attribution, although building work was going on at the time in the Stableyard. Equally, there is no documentary evidence for the more recently propounded theory that the staircase and panelling (at least) date from the alterations of the 1870s undertaken by Charles Langton-Massingberd, when such exact revivals of early 18th-century forms were fashionable.

Lady Montgomery-Massingberd (b.1872) certainly believed in the antiquity – and the quality – of her staircase. If guests complained of the cold, to warm them up she advised a good spell on their hands and knees polishing it.

Portraits

The gallery of family portraits hanging here includes Peregrine Langton by Schiavone (which was painted in Venice in 1843 during Charles and Harriet Langton Massingberd's honeymoon there), Emily Langton Massingberd by T.B. Wirgman (with her violin), her husband, Edmund Langton (by the same) and each of their children: Mildred (by J.C. Moore) Stephen and Mary (by Moore) and Diana (by Wirgman).

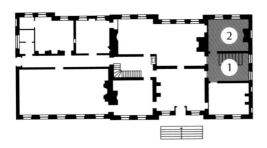

Opposite **The Oak Staircase**
Below **The Study**

Up on the landing is rather a poor likeness of Charles Langton-Massingberd, who rescued Gunby from the wreck of 'Naughty' Algernon's extravagances. A better portrait of him hangs in the Dining Room. The connection of Mr and Mrs Parker to Gunby – in Tudor dress and over-cleaned – is unknown.

Furniture

The massive oak chair with hefty ring-turned supports and the initials of Emily Langton Massingberd carved into the back, is typical of the attempts to supply the burgeoning taste for 'old oak' furniture at the end of the 19th century. This example is particularly crude and was probably made locally specifically for presentation to Emily. The real thing (late 16th-/early 17th-century) can be seen by the fireplace in the Entrance Hall.

2. The Study

Historically, this was the Morning Room, catching the early sun from the east. Now it houses the considerable military library belonging to Field Marshal Sir Archibald Montgomery-Massingberd. The Field Marshal was an author of some repute on his own account, writing the history of the Fourth Army in the 'Hundred Days' of 1918 and publishing tracts on strategy and tactics as well as a slim volume of autobiography. There are also reminders of his Indian postings in the lacquered bottles and jugs he brought back with him. The watercolours and prints include scenes of game birds by Archibald Thorburn taken on the Gunby Estate.

Pranks in armour

The suit of armour features in Hugh Montgomery-Massingberd's *Daydream Believer* in a prank designed to ridicule a local news story of ghosts at Gunby. He and a group of friends in fancy dress (including the armour) went down to the gate and paraded round the roundabout on the main road, 'gurning and grimacing' until 'the traffic was brought to a complete standstill'. His father was quite amused, but Rogers the caretaker was not, barring the door and calling the police.

The Dining Room

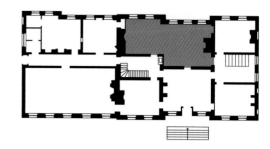

The shape of this room has altered too. When Charles Langton Massingberd added the North Wing containing a dining room, this space was created out of the old Dining Room and Butler's Pantry to act as a Drawing Room. Sentimental epithets carved into the fireplace and on the lintel mix uneasily with pious injunctions and quotations from Shakespeare. A homely note is struck by the use of a couple of old bed posts to mark the former division. A few years later, with the creation of the Music Room, this space reverted to its former use.

Portraits

Elizabeth Mary Anne Massingberd presides over the south fireplace, facing her uncle Thomas at the north. On the right is the ethereal portrait of Margaret Massingberd, painted at Gunby in 1903 by Arthur Hughes. Vernon Lushington, Margaret's father, reported in a letter from Gunby dated 12 July, to his youngest daughter Susan:

'Here I am at Gunby, playing master of the house to Mr Hughes, for Margaret & Stephen are away at Belton … Dear Mr Hughes is enraptured with the place, the house, the garden, & Margaret, Stephen – everybody, & everything. I hope he may so continue, it will help him to paint his picture. This he has not begun, but showed me of his free will, a sketch he had made for his design – Margaret in the garden, a little bit of the house showing, and flowers & white doves. He says it will be "decorative".'

On the left is Margaret's sister-in-law, Diana, with her viola. This was painted during the Second World War by Richard Ziegler, an exile from Germany who took refuge at Gunby. He wrote home to his wife describing the creation of this portrait and sketching it for her in the letter. A further portrait of Lady Montgomery-Massingberd, by Sir Oswald Birley, hangs nearby and was disliked by its sitter nearly as much as its companion of the Field Marshal her husband (illustrated on p.18), which, she complained, 'makes him look like a beery old man!' This was condemnation indeed from such a stalwart devotee of the temperance movement.

Further round the room 'Naughty' Algernon, who brought the family finances to the brink of disaster, smirks on a rocky shore resplendent in his naval uniform. His be-whiskered Uncle Charles, entirely unacquainted with smirking, hangs nearby.

Furniture

The two sets of dining chairs are both good examples of the refined forms of early Regency taste, with sabre legs and caned seats. One set is painted with lions' masks, whilst the other exhibits the sun disc of Amun Ra carved on its cresting rails and is an example of Egyptian Revival taste. The marquetry longcase clock is by Matthew Bunce, who probably died very shortly after making this clock in about 1700.

Below The Dining Room

A Lady's Accomplishment

In the crook of the main room is a standard corner cupboard. At a cursory glance it is made of lacquer. With two seconds scrutiny it is obviously not, and with a little more investigation it becomes clear that it is indeed that rare survival, a Lady's Accomplishment. In the era when women of aristocratic and landowning status could not work for a living, the outlets for their skills and creativity were few. Gardening, embroidery, music, painting and drawing were amongst those accomplishments considered suitable for a lady of rank. Devising and working in decorative terms was an advanced skill which few accomplished to any great standard. Elizabeth Mary Anne appears to have made gallant attempts to join the exalted ranks of the truly skilled amateur. Her charming designs for pergolas, gate piers and even gate lodges survive in her sketch book. Her attempts at japanning survive also on this corner cupboard. Sadly, her enthusiastic application of gilt transfer borders and plaster squeezes of little chinamen in haphazard pavilions is rather heavy and misses the essential lightness and fantasy of true chinoiseries by some way. Nevertheless the importance to Gunby of having this evidence of Elizabeth Mary Anne's bid for artistic accomplishment is very precious. In her DIY treatment of this ordinary piece of furniture much is revealed about her, her life and the era in which she lived.

Above The Dining Room mantelpiece is inscribed 'Love and Friendship mingle in the Ingle-Nook'

Miniatures

The miniatures over the south mantel show, amongst others, Sir Henry Massingberd (who had his Commonwealth title re-conferred by King Charles II), Henry Massingberd (father of Elizabeth Mary Anne, whose bookplate is to be found all over the Library) and Charles Langton Massingberd (twice, once in the uniform of an Austrian hussar).

The Backstairs
The Squire's Bedroom
The Grey Bedroom
The Field Marshal's Bedroom
The Cedar Bedroom
The Sitting Room
The Blue Bathroom

Below **The Cedar Bedroom**

1. The Backstairs

This staircase rises from the Basement to the top floor and connects the 1873 North Wing to the old house. It is decorated for much of its height in the 'Daisy' pattern wallpaper designed by William Morris and printed for the first time in 1864 by Jeffrey & Co. The charcoal sketches of the three Lushington sisters are preparatory drawings for the painting *The Home Quartette* that Vernon Lushington commissioned from Arthur Hughes. A modern print of the painting hangs above.

The drawing of the head of Margaret Lushington is by William Holman Hunt. Both Hunt and Hughes are considered amongst the most talented painters of the Pre-Raphaelite circle.

2. The Squire's Bedroom

Turning left on the landing down the little passage, be sure to note the very striking portrait of the charismatic preacher Damian de Veuster. Also apparent is the innovative way in which bathrooms were introduced into the junction between the old and new wings. The Squire's Room has wallpaper of an Asiatic pattern in the panels.

4. The Field Marshal's Bedroom

The large sepia photograph over the mantel is of Raphael's *Sistine Madonna* and is typical of the taste of an artistically minded household of the late 19th century. Behind the door is a fine 'seaweed' marquetry bureau bookcase of the early 18th century. The marquetry pattern of arabesques is cut into the walnut veneer with great skill. This piece was left to Gunby by Freda Massingberd-Campbell, the daughter of Alice, who was the younger sister of Emily. Freda passed much of the Second World War in the south of France. Her diaries for part of that period remain at Gunby.

5. The Cedar Bedroom

On the south-west corner of the house, this must have been the most favoured of the bedrooms. Its carved 'Greek key' overmantel panel is probably one of the improvements introduced by William Meux Massingberd in the 1730s.

6. The Sitting Room

Situated over the front door, this room would have been the primary bedchamber of Sir William Massingberd's new house in 1700. Given a modish bed alcove and a new doorway onto the staircase landing in the Regency upgrading of the house by Elizabeth Mary Anne Massingberd, it became a private sitting room for Mr and Mrs Wrisdale in the 1970s, when Lawrence Bond altered the fireplace and restored the original entrance to the room.

7. The Blue Bathroom

Across the landing is the Bathroom, containing a curious ebonised and gilt cabinet mounted with two different sets of blue and white tiles, very much in the 'Aesthetic' taste of the 1890s. Outside, the walls are covered with a rare Morris & Co. red pomegranate-pattern paper. The National Trust had some of this reprinted to cover an area destroyed by earlier electrical work. The 'Loo with a View' is a great favourite.

Above **The Field Marshal's Bedroom**

Below left **The decorated washstand in the Bathroom**

This dates from *c*.1920, is of very poor quality and is in irreparable condition.

3. The Grey Bedroom

The utilitarian treatment of the fireplace must date from alterations in the late 19th century. The wallpaper, however, dates from 1928.

The commode, or night stool, is a beautifully crafted piece of deceptive furniture, with a hinged dummy front that lifts to reveal the padded seat and back rest (both are rare and fragile survivals – please do not sit!).

In a house full of prints and engravings of all sorts, the copper engraving (hanging between the windows) of a 17th-century French politician is one of the finest. Look at the hair of the wig and see how it is made up of thousands of minutely observed strokes of the engraver's burin.

The Basement

The Basement runs under the entire house, mimicking the plan of the main apartments above, thus the coal cellar is under the Entrance Hall (the blocked chutes for the delivery of the coal are visible behind the roses to the right of the steps) the old Kitchen is under the Dining Room, and the Servants' Hall is under the Music Room.

Retrenchment after the war led to the abandonment of the Old Kitchen and the creation of a new Kitchen nearer the Dining Room upstairs. The Old Kitchen retains a few pieces of furniture that would have been made on the estate such as the table and the deep sets of drawers. More sophisticated items, such as the haster (or warming cupboard) set on casters for rolling in front of the fire, would have been brought in. The remains of the last cast-iron range were discovered, completely rusted away, when the inglenook was opened early in the 1990s.

The addition of the North Wing in 1873 greatly expanded the service areas Below Stairs and enabled the redistribution of tasks to different areas; the larder was established under the stairs (rather perversely) on the south front of the house with the Still Room, complete with its own range, to the east. Here tea was made for the household whilst the main Kitchen was taken up with the preparation of dinner. In addition this was where the preserves, jams and chutneys were made in season from fruit and vegetables from the garden. The space occupied by the

Above left **The Game Larder**

Left **Julian Maudit's** *c.*1720 recipe for pickling oysters

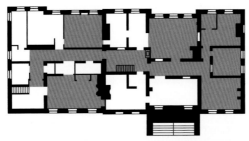

Above right The servants' bells in the Service Corridor

second-hand bookshop offered cellarage for beer, with wines housed under slightly greater security further along the corridor.

The Game Charts on the walls of the corridor are a reminder that the estate, as well as being agricultural, was always a sporting estate.

The Servants' Hall was a spacious room, in which all the servants ate together. Gunby's establishment, even at its height, was not grand or numerous enough to warrant separate eating arrangements for the upper servants. Don't miss the two watercolours of the Hall, both from the west, one showing the place c.1800 and the other c.1730 (although, stylistically and subjectively, a date later in the century seems more likely).

Across the corridor in rooms that comprised the male servants' sleeping accommodation, and latterly formed part of a flat, is an exhibition devoted to the military career of Field Marshal Sir Archibald Montgomery-Massingberd. Here are tiger skin rugs from India, drawings by Lockwood Kipling (Rudyard's father), many photographs and watercolours of the campaigns in which Sir Archie was involved, and the portrait by Birley so disliked by Lady Montgomery-Massingberd.

You should leave via the steps at the end of the corridor up to the North Courtyard.

The Gardens

'…and enable me to make pleasant shady walks for the summer all around the mansion. Nothing can be more charming and delightful than the prospect of so many pretty rising plantations….'
Peregrine Massingberd's Journal for 1811/12

Above The clock was a present from Susan Lushington to her brother-in-law Stephen Massingberd in 1917

Opposite Gunby is famous for its richly planted herbaceous borders

It is apparent from the number of men, described as gardeners, who were being paid to come from London in the period 1700–10 that a garden was being created (the building of the wall on the south side of the 'East Garden' is identifiable in a bill of 1707). However, certain features such as the formal canal suggest pre-existing gardens associated with the former manor house.

Whether any of the garden walls predate 1700 is uncertain, but it is likely they were largely as we see them today quite early in the garden's development. The dovecot and Gardens Cottage were probably early arrivals too.

A barn was built north of the Hall in 1730, but it was in 1735/6 that the series of fine stables and coach houses seen today were built by William Meux Massingberd. The clock was a present from Susan Lushington to her brother-in-law Stephen Massingberd in 1917.

The first concrete evidence for the form of the gardens appears in plans drawn in that unique record, the Gunby Tree Book. Although started earlier, the book was brought into extensive use by Peregrine in 1804 to record his works, plantings and improvements over the whole estate, including the gardens. Beautifully drawn plans of the walled kitchen garden, the offices of the North Courtyard (which he improved) and the south and east gardens adorn the text. In addition, his finished watercolour of the west front of the Hall shows an arrangement of screen walls with arched doorways and an oval gravelled sweep that is confirmed by the tithe map of 1837.

His plan of the Walled Garden shows the main vegetable garden much as it appears now with four main plots divided by axial paths. The current position of the great herbaceous border facing the east lawn is taken up with a Melon Ground and a pond. Behind the wall in the current Pergola Garden are mushroom sheds, grape houses and a massive dung heap situated directly behind the stables.

From the Tree Book it is plain that Peregrine felt the last tenants of the Hall had treated the garden very poorly: the plan of the south garden is annotated 'When Lord Gwydir and Lady Willoughby rent'd this place (1785 to 1800) they destroy'd the gardens especially this Flower Garden …'. The plan shows the east lawn considerably smaller than now, with a diagonal boundary (in 1806 a 'double hedge') running across it to the park boundary south of the Hall. The tithe map of 1837 shows this detail softened to a gentle curve ending on the western edge of the pond. Charles Langton Massingberd extended the lawn east to its current dimensions, recorded in a watercolour of his in 1865.

A formal garden probably existed on the west front of the Hall in the early 1700s, but this had probably gone by c.1735 according to a painting that is dated to that period. The current layout of yew topiary dates from 1902/3 (see p.44–5).

The Pergola Garden

There is no prescribed 'tour' of Gunby's gardens, but many like to start through the discreet gate at the north-east corner of the house into the dark shadow of centenarian yews. Emerging onto the lawn under the ancient Cedar of Lebanon, the Pergola Garden is announced by a pair of lead urns filled with pelargoniums on the left. These, supported by broad herbaceous borders lead to a brick arch which proceeds to the pergola beyond. This is in a series of simple supports, over which apple trees, including varieties 'James Grieve' and 'Kings Acre Pippin' dating back to a list compiled in 1944, are trained in tightly pruned formation.

The walled compartment which the pergola bisects contains the cutting border, a rose garden, the yellow border and a herb garden. To the left the herbs (over 80 of them) have been re-arranged around a central stone trough by Betty Wrisdale and her Head Gardener, Paul Gray. Both culinary and medicinal varieties reflect usage in a country house of the scale of Gunby.

The roses to the right include yellows and oranges 'Chinatown', 'Arthur Bell' and 'Graham Stuart Thomas' (the last, according to its namesake, likes 'to be pruned very hard') with reds 'Frensham', 'Wilhelm' and 'Orange Triumph' (which is, nonetheless, red).

The little box-edged lawn with its central sundial was probably laid out around 1900 by Margaret Massingberd, who also brought the little domed seat from elsewhere in the gardens as part of her replanning of this area.

'Our England is a garden,
and such gardens are not made
by singing, "O! How beautiful!"
and sitting in the shade.'

Rudyard Kipling,
The Glory of the Garden, 1911

Dovecots were a common feature of country house estates from medieval times. Young doves (or 'squabs') were harvested from the nesting boxes which line the walls internally and put to culinary use. Gunby's dovecot retains its fixed ladder set on a revolving mechanism (a 'potence') that gives easy access to the squabs.

Honeysuckle embowers the seat and frames the view of the mixed herbaceous border on the other side of the lawn.

The cutting borders run down to the greenhouses either side of the pergola. Here the flowers that light up the Hall in traditional arrangements of loose abandon are grown (there is no better place in England in which to experience summer bowls of sweet peas censing the rooms with their heavy perfume than at Gunby). The house is supplied throughout the season with an endless variety of colour and form. In the greenhouses many types of pelargonium, regal and zonal, including the unusual *Stella*, are nurtured, brought to flowering perfection, sent in and then cosseted back to floral health following a sojourn in the Dining Room jardinière. The square brick building dominating the garden's easterly aspect is the dovecot. This is as old as the Hall (possibly older) and retains its resident flock of doves.

The Yellow Border

The Yellow Border is a double herbaceous border featuring unusual plants such as *Buphthalmum speciosum*, a large-headed yellow daisy, *Achillea* 'Cloth of Gold' and *Ligularia clivorum* 'Desdemona', another daisy, but orange this time with leaves suffused with purple. At the end, the arched gateway on the left leads past Kipling's couplet, immortalised in stone, into the Kitchen Garden.

Left Long view through the Pergola

The Kitchen Garden

'It is this profuse combination of seasonable fruits and flowers …
that invests Gunby with the air of a still living English country home'.

James Lees-Milne, Gunby guidebook, 1946

It appears that of all the areas of the gardens at Gunby, the Kitchen Garden has altered least in appearance and usage over time. The cross-axial paths dividing the four main compartments and the linking perimeter path are all in evidence in Peregrine Massingberd's plan of 1806 in the Tree Book. In the heyday of the gardens, then and ever since, the four compartments and wall beds have been in vegetable production. The fruit trees on the garden walls were listed in 1806 and include White Magdalen peach, brown fig (against the dovecot) Chaumontelle pear, Temple Nectrine, Nutmeg Peach and Breda Apricot. Today, pears, plums, gages and figs clothe the walls, with apples and more pears creating a rhythm down the central double herbaceous border. Colours progress from blues to oranges and reds, and back to blues and whites with the seasons. Roses, a gift to Lady Montgomery-Massingberd in 1962, form the cross axis. These include the Pemberton hybrid musk roses 'Penelope', 'Cornelia' and 'Prosperity', famous for their heavy scent, which is at its

Below left Marrow frames in the vegetable garden

Below right Fruit and vegetables from the garden can be bought in season

best in the cool of a summer's evening. The vegetable crops are rotated around the wall borders, and the fruit and vegetables are available for purchase in season, whilst a proportion is used in the tea-room.

Instead of a wall on the south side, a yew hedge divides the Kitchen Garden from the canal. Irish juniper trees punctuate the formal line of the walk, which is known as the Ghost Walk. A young woman of the Massingberd family died after the murder of her stable lad lover by her infuriated father. Her ghost is said to walk here. The dying boy's curse is supposed to be responsible for the remarkably few occasions in the history of Gunby that the succession has passed directly from father to son. The canal is a formal feature that seems curiously misplaced, without any relationship to the house or other features of the garden.

This suggests that it may survive from the garden of the previous manor house. In the past it has been used as a holding pond for fish brought in from the park ponds for use in the kitchens.

Passing through the double iron gates into evergreen gloom, the path to the church runs straight on whilst two walks wind round to the right. One leads back up the south side of the canal, whilst the other, left-hand one leads into a cherry walk, first planted in 1939. Only one of the original trees survives, a *Pyrus malus*. Re-planting has included a Great White, *Prunus serrulata* 'Tai-haku', which, in 1987, marked the 60th anniversary of the National Gardens Scheme, of which Gunby was an original supporter. The surprise view of the east front of the house leads onto the East Lawn.

Above *The Ghost Walk*; watercolour by Caroline Grosvenor

The East Lawn

The uninterrupted view of the east front of the house is framed by some fine specimen trees, a black mulberry, a robinia and a liquidambar as well as a couple of cedars, all planted in the last couple of decades to provide succession to trees that have been lost during the 20th century.

In the shrubbery to the left *Rosa cantabrigiensis* makes a show, with 'Wedding Day' clambering through the holly behind.

Behind this shrubbery is a spring flower walk snaking its serpentine way along the park boundary. In season it is bright with winter aconites, snowdrops, crocuses and primroses.

The carpet of wood anemones is particularly beautiful in March and April. The old horse chestnut tree, probably the sole survivor of Peregrine's semi-circular walk adjacent to his new Flower Garden, is venerable but has dropped branches in the recent past. In 1904 a tennis lawn (as it is referred to) was created here due south of the house. On the East Lawn, a pair of box-edged beds holds hybrid tea roses 'Mrs Oakley Fisher' and the heavily scented 'Etoile de Hollande'. The planting of the great Cedar of Lebanon is recorded in the Tree Book in 1812.

Above A Cedar of Lebanon at Gunby painted by Charles Langton Massingberd in 1875

Opposite The West Garden

The West Garden

The current formal planting of a pair of parallel yew allées dates from 1902/3 with a stone walk centrally leading to a sundial formed of a baluster from old Kew Bridge. Reputedly the gate piers on the drive were moved here from the site of the moated manor house at Bratoft in 1948.

In his plan of his new Flower Garden drawn in 1806, Peregrine sketches a number of individual trees just to the west of the garden and cut off from it by the wing wall. The trees noted include '... six Yews in the original old Garden. Planted about the year 1700'. It is probably one of these that survives adjacent to the south-west corner of the tennis lawn. Just a little further south, a note on the drawing, signed and dated, states 'The Stables formerly stood near this spot'. Brick rubble under the yew hedges and cobbles discovered when replanting the catmint suggests an older use of this area. Certainly Peregrine seemed convinced that a formal garden used to stand between the house and the public road which used to follow a north–south course on the parish boundary about 20m beyond the western edge of the garden. So, the current formal layout of English and Irish yews might well echo an 18th-century predecessor with greater accuracy than its creator, Margaret Massingberd, could ever have imagined. The golden privet balls in the corners and lavender and catmint sprawling over the path however, are entirely 20th-century innovations.

On the walls of the house 'Sylvia' and 'Madame Butterfly' vie for eminence, whilst back in the Courtyard the vigorous 'Mermaid' (a single yellow rose) climbs up by the little gate in the corner, and a rarity, 'Breeze Hill', swoons on the clock tower opposite in big cabbage roses of pinkish apricot.

The Estate

'This estate is extraordinarily feudal, and has an air of wellbeing and content.'
James Lees-Milne, *Diaries*, 15 June 1945

The size of the estate at Gunby has fluctuated wildly. At its height in the late 17th century, land ownership extended as far as the east coast. A gradual decline, brought on by minority successions and absentee ownership, accelerated dramatically as a result of the brief tenure of Algernon Massingberd in the mid-19th century. His gambling and hare-brained schemes for getting rich combined with his progressive, if rather muddled, espousal of ultra-democratic political causes spelled disaster for the traditional agricultural estate he had inherited. By the time his uncle had finished paying off his debts, the estate was so much diminished that it no longer stretched more than a few miles from the Hall in any direction, let alone the nine miles to the coast, where the bustling holiday resort of Skegness was to be developed on former Massingberd land.

It is fortunate, perhaps, that Algernon's grandfather, Peregrine Massingberd, had been a keen student of landscape gardening with a particular love of trees and a strong desire to bequeath a thriving estate and a beautiful landscape to his heirs. Whilst his own financial incompetence made the former unlikely, we are the lucky beneficiaries of his marked success in the latter.

Planting with an eye for grandeur and extent, Peregrine benefited from the advice of his friend, the nurseryman and landscape gardener William Pontey. Pontey had published a series of books, culminating in *The Rural Improver* of 1822.

Expanding on the theories of 'Capability' Brown, his favourite device was to select a distant architectural feature on which to focus the view and plant so that the subject became framed by umbrageous woodland when seen from the appointed viewpoint. At Gunby the viewpoint was always the house. Whilst some of the views have become obscured by the expansion and growth of the gardens, others – to local church towers and farmsteads – still work from the perimeter. In a flat terrain such as Gunby's, the impression given today of an extensive and generously wooded landscape, far greater than actually exists, is a triumphant vindication of Pontey's theories.

Peregrine devised other improvements, creating a raised walk along the edge of his estate looking south east across Magdalen College's land and north and east across his wife's domain. This he linked to the Hall via Ice House Pond where he created a little woodland garden. The National Trust has begun to restore this garden and its links to the Hall.

Green lanes criss-cross the estate, linking Gunby with Bratoft. Both villages have atrophied over the past few centuries, Gunby largely surviving as archaeological mounds in the park just beyond the church. It is one of many deserted medieval villages in a county where the population never recovered after sheep farming replaced subsistence agriculture in the later Middle Ages. These remains, and the even more mysterious ones at Bratoft, await further investigation.

The site of the moated manor house at Bratoft has been a destination for visitors to Gunby for many generations. Recent research has begun to uncover exciting indications of an Elizabethan water garden. There was an extensive walled park at Bratoft. At Gunby the park stood initially at just 40 acres before growing to the south and east of the house, taking advantage of Peregrine and Pontey's plantations to gain greater apparent volume. A short-lived new drive from the east was formed, coming into the park at Old Lodge Farm, but no evidence has been found of it ever having reached the Hall.

Charles Langton Massingberd rebuilt the churches at Gunby and Bratoft, as well as a number of the farms and cottages (even in its severely reduced state Gunby had some ten tenanted farming units at the end of the 19th century. These are now farmed together in three tenancies.) His daughter Emily built the Red House on Burgh Road and Acacia Cottage in Bratoft, and her son Stephen built Gowthams Cottages in Gunby and replaced the gate lodge designed by Elizabeth Mary Anne Massingberd with an Oetzmann's cottage bought at the Franco-British Exhibition in 1908. The surviving example of Elizabeth Mary Anne's *cottage ornée* designing can be seen near the church and Manor Farm (a fine 17th-century farmhouse) in Bratoft.

A rare survival of a Lincolnshire 'mud and stud' thatched cottage at Whitegates is available as a holiday cottage, sleeping just two, whereas the rather grander Rectory at Bratoft can accommodate up to eleven. In the gardens Orchard Cottage offers accommodation for up to four people.

The Massingberds of Gunby

Thomas Massingberd = Frances Habton
(1562–1636) of Bratoft and Gunby

Sir Henry Massingberd, 1st Bt* = (2) Anne Stoughton (*née* Evans)
(1609–80) of Bratoft and Gunby

Sir Drayner Massingberd,
ancestor of the Massingberd-Mundys of Ormsby

Sir William Massingberd, 2nd Bt* = Elizabeth Wynn
(1649-1719) of Bratoft and Gunby

Sir William Massingberd, 3rd and last Bt*
(1677-1723) of Gunby;
MP for Lincolnshire

Elizabeth Meux Massingberd* = Thomas Meux
(*d.* 1738) of Gunby

William Meux Massingberd = (1) Mary Thornborough*
(1703–81) of Gunby   (2) Elizabeth Drake (*d.* 1771)

William (*d.* 1734)   Thomas Massingberd* (*d.* 1777) = Elizabeth Emerson (*d.* 1812)

Henry Massingberd* = Elizabeth Hoare
(*d.* 1784) of Gunby

Captain Thomas Massingberd RN* of Candlesbury, ancestor of the Finnish and Yorkshire
branches of the family (which include the Harrogate car group, Massingberds)

Elizabeth Langton Massingberd* = Peregrine Langton, later Langton Massingberd* (*d.* 1856)
(1783–1835) of Gunby   (Son of Bennet Langton) m. 1802

Rev. Algernon = Catherine   Samuel   Henry   **Mary*** = Hastings Neville   **Charles Langton** = (1) Harriet Langford*   Margaret
Langton Massingberd* Pearce*   (1805-14)   (1806-17)   (1807-51)   m. 1831   **Massingberd*** (2) Harriet Newman   (*d.* 1837)
(1804–44) of Gunby   (1815–87) of Gunby

Algernon Massingberd*
(1828–55) of Gunby

Emily Langton Massingberd* = Edmund Langton*
(1847–97) of Gunby

Major Stephen = Margaret   **Mildred*** = Major Leonard   **Mary*** = Major-General Hugh   **Diana** = Field-Marshal
Massingberd* Lushington*   (1868–1941) Darwin (son of   (1871–1950) Montgomery of   **Montgomery-** Sir Archbald
(1869–1925)   (*d.* 1906)   of Gunby   Charles Darwin)   Blessingbourne,   **Massingberd*** Montgomery-
of Gunby   m. 1900   Co. Tyrone   (1872–1963) Massingberd*
                                                 m. 1894   of Gunby   (1871-1947)
                                                                     m. 1896

John Montgomery-Massingberd* = Marsoli Winlaw (*née* Seal)
(1913–2004)   (1912–2004)

Hugh Montgomery-Massingberd* = (1) Christine Martinoni
(1946–2007)   (2) Caroline Ripley

Mary

Luke (b. 1977) = Maria-Alexandra Vargas Fandiño   Harriet = (1) Gareth Jenkins

Santiago (b. 2010)   Federico (b. 2012)   Jack (b. 2005)   Hugo (b. 2009)   * Denotes a portrait at Gunby